Lighting The Flame

A Resource Book
For Worship

Chuck Cammarata

CSS Publishing Company, Inc., Lima, Ohio

Library of Congress Cataloging-in-Publication Data

Cammarata, Chuck, 1957-
   Lighting the flame : a resource book for worship / Chuck Cammarata.
     p. cm.
   ISBN 0-7880-0870-6
   1. Pastoral prayers. 2. Gathering rites—Texts. 3. Confession (Prayer) I. Title.
BV250.C594   1997
264'.13—dc20
                                             96-38669
                                               CIP

This book is available in the following formats, listed by ISBN:
     0-7880-0870-6   Book
     0-7880-0898-6   Mac
     0-7880-0899-4   IBM 3 1/2
     0-7880-1003-4   Sermon Prep

This book was possible only because of the gracious and open spirit of the people of the Fairview Presbyterian Church who willingly embraced liturgy that was new and sometimes a bit provoking. I could not have been blessed with a more receptive first congregation. To all my brothers and sisters in Christ in my family at Fairview, this book is dedicated. Thank you for being my friends rather than my parishioners.

Table Of Contents

Introduction

We've all been to worship services where the liturgy has been an exercise in irrelevance and boredom. It ought not to be that way. Liturgy ought to be the spark that lights the fire of worship. It can, if appropriate attention is given it, touch hearts as deeply as a sonorous anthem or an inspiring sermon. For liturgy to accomplish that though, it needs to be fresh, thought-provoking, passionate, varied, and real.

Over the ten years that I have been preparing liturgy for worship, I have tried hard to imbue it with each of those qualities. It works in our church. People are often as touched by the prayers and responses as by the sermon. (I hope that is not due to Sominex sermons!) For several years now, many in our congregation have been encouraging me to share my liturgies with other pastors. Now, thanks to CSS, I am being allowed to do that. My hope is that other pastors and congregations might benefit from the liturgies in this book, and the ones they will inspire others to write.

I want to acknowledge two very special people as part of this introduction. First, to my friend Chuck Crist, a retired pastor who has done more listening to me than I had a right to expect him to do, and who encouraged me to seek out a publisher for my liturgies, I want to say thank you for your tolerance and love. And to my wonderful wife Donna who toiled many long hours over this manuscript, and who loves me always. I want to say, even though this may not be the most appropriate format, I am more grateful for your love and support than you will ever know. I love you.

To all of you who are using this book, I hope this small effort to enliven worship, to "Light the Flame" of worship, will be a useful blessing to you. Let us worship God!

Chapter 1

General Liturgies

Calls To Worship

Awesome God
Call To Worship

Leader: Our God is an awesome God,

People: A God who makes trees and moves mountains,

Leader: A God who decides the rise and fall of nations,

People: A God who rules the fury of the thunderstorm,

Leader: A God who seeks the lost lamb,

People: A God who heals the sick,

Leader: A God who loves even the sinner,

People: Our God is an awesome God.

Leader: Let us worship our God.

Church
Call To Worship

Leader: So, you're going to church again, huh?

People: Yeah, it helps me. Why don't you come with me?

Leader: Nah, just a bunch of hypocrites there.

People: Yeah, but lovable ones.

Leader: I suppose, but no thanks. It's all just a waste of time.

People: Not for me. Don't you ever feel like you need a little inspiration? Like your batteries need charged? Isn't your heart ever hungry for God's touch? Don't you ever feel the need just to say thank you for all your blessings?

Leader: Well, yeah, I guess I do sometimes.

People: That's what church is for. Are you sure you don't want to come?

Leader: Let us worship God!

In Need
Call To Worship

Leader: We come today, Lord, some of us,
     with gladness and joy in our hearts,

People: Grateful for your good gifts!

Leader: We come today, Lord, others of us,
　　　　angry, anxious, frustrated,
People: Pursuing the peace only you can give.
Leader: We come today, Lord, broken, bruised, battered,
People: Hoping to be healed by the Great Physician.
Leader: We come worn and weary,
People: Seeking the strength of your spirit.
Leader: Be to us all, Lord, on this day of new mercies,
　　　　be to us the God we need you to be.
People: Calm us, heal us, revive us, love us.
Leader: Come, let us worship God! Amen.

Passages

Call To Worship
Leader: Life is full of passages,
People: Full of moving on to new stages of life,
Leader: Full of leaving behind the old and familiar;
People: The first day of school,
Leader: The first date,
People: Graduation, marriage, children, growing old, and all the rest.
Leaders: And each stage is pregnant with possibilities,
People: Possibilities of triumph and joy, or defeat and sorrow,
Leader: Wonderful possibilities, frightening possibilities.
People: But onward into the possibilities we must go.
Leader: Always remembering, though, that through every passage, into each new stage of life, our God goes with us,
People: Quietly pointing the way to wholeness,
Leader: Patiently finding us when we get lost,
People: Lovingly lifting us when we fail and fall.
Leader: So, let us prepare for the possibilities of tomorrow by worshipping God today.
People: Hallelujah!
Leader: Praise the Lord!

12

Peace, Love, Grace

Call To Worship

Leader: May the peace of God rest upon our busy lives,

People: That we may be quieted into prayer.

Leader: May the love of God flow through our worship,

People: That we may be enlivened with opportunities to serve.

Leader: May the grace of God seek out our every need,

People: That the restless gospel may set our hearts afire.

Leader: Amen!

People: Amen!

Worship The Lord

Call To Worship

Leader: Come, worship the Lord.

People: He is great and glorious.

Leader: He is majestic and magnificent.

People: He is an awesome God!

Leader: Come, let us worship the Lord.

People: His is a gentle and tender touch.

Leader: His mercy moves hard hearts to tears.

People: His love heals our brokenness.

Leader: Come, let us worship the Lord!

Prayers Of Confession

Abundant Life

Prayer Of Confession

Leader: A great feast is laid out before your eyes,
To bring your five senses vibrantly alive;
Pastas, pizza, meats, and marinades,
Your grandmother's pumpkin pie,
Stuffing and turkey, and hams and yams,
Food that will make your tongue cry.

And juices, and punches, and nectar like wine,
    A meal unbelievably fine.
And it's offered each day, on the corner of life,
    By a man who seems strangely divine.
People: **But people passed by, without even a glance.**
    His banquet was sampled by few.
Leader: Though they hungered and thirsted
    For this food of life,
        Its delight they never knew.
People: **The great sin of all time,**
    Is that he offers us life,
    But we choose existence instead.
Leader: When will we learn to dine at his feast,
    and be alive, not among the walking dead?

Busyness
Prayer Of Confession
Leader: Lord, how is it possible that we live so little of our lives consciously in your company?
People: **Our minds, our hearts, our senses are focused so often on the minor.**
Leader: We have so many things to do.
People: **Hurry up and eat! We're going to be late for the ball game!**
Leader: I won't be home for dinner tonight, honey, I've got a meeting.
People: **Piano and dance; and soccer and softball;**
Leader: And Mission and Nurture; and Trustees and Deacons;
People: **And AAUW and Church Women United; and PTO and Brownies;**
Leader: And on and on and on. O Lord, how have we let it come to this?
People: **Help us focus on those things that are primary.**
Leader: Help us to find the courage to sit at your feet and soak up your wisdom, and love, and power.
People: **Help us, Lord, help us! Amen!**

Change

Prayer Of Confession

Leader: The survey concluded: "After age thirty, people just don't change much."

People: Our proverbs say, "You can't teach an old dog new tricks."

Leader: We become cynics who think nothing and no one can change,

People: People who mouth the words, "Our God makes all things new again," but don't really believe them.

Leader: And yet we know that winter does give way to spring,

People: That once in a while, somehow, things do change,

Leader: Sauls become Pauls,
Berlin walls fall,
A Rosa Parks stands tall,
Hard hearts thaw,
and something is changed.

People: O Lord, we believe, we want to believe.
Help thou our unbelief. Amen.

Conflict

Prayer Of Confession

Leader: Sometimes I'd rather not come to church.

People: Really? Why?

Leader: Because sometimes I'd rather not face some of you.

People: Don't you like us?

Leader: That's not it at all. I love you.

People: Then what is it?

Leader: Well, sometimes I've had some conflict with some of you, and sometimes I've done something or said something I shouldn't have and ...

People: And you'd rather avoid us.

Leader: Something like that.

People: Because you don't like conflict, and you'd rather not face the uncomfortable feelings that often go with having made mistakes.

Leader: Yes, you're right.

People: O Lord, forgive us this weakness that would rather run and avoid than face the music of our mistakes and differences. Help us to be a forgiving community; a place where we can come in our weakness and brokenness and find support; a people who heal one another rather than wound each other. Help us to be, Lord Jesus, all you would have us be as your church in this place. Amen.

Detachment
Prayer Of Confession

O God, we really don't want to see the slums, the war, the poverty, the hatred, the sickness in our world or in ourselves. We are afraid to see, afraid to think, to feel, to care. Help us to trust in you and your strength that we might begin to see and care, and in so doing rediscover the depths of life which enable us to be truly and fully alive. Amen.

Failure To Love
Prayer Of Confession

Leader: Lord, we confess that we have not given our full attention to primary matters.

People: You have told us, "Love our neighbors."

Leader: We have ignored them.

People: You have told us, "Love ourselves."

Leader: We have despised our gifts and hated ourselves.

People: You have told us to selflessly use our lives.

Leader: We have selfishly kept our lives for ourselves.

People: We failed you, our neighbors, and ourselves. Forgive us!

Leader: Lord, as we repent, turn us toward a better way,

People: Your way of self-respect, love for others, and selfless service. Amen!

Hiding

Prayer Of Confession

Leader: Lord, when hard times come, we run.

People: We lose confidence in you.

Leader: We hide and try to calm our fears with drugs, or relationships, or new starts in new places.

People: We hope and pray that our troubles won't find us.

Leader: But they find us, always they find us, for the troubles really are in us.

People: The troubles' sources are our self-centeredness, or our fear of being alone, or our anger, or self-hatred.

Leader: And there are no places to hide from ourselves.

People: Only you can provide the strength we need to face the world and its trials.

Leader: Only you can provide the power we need to face ourselves and the darkness of our souls.

People: Only in you can we find the peace we need.

Leader: Lord, help us to hide in you and you alone, that we might be victorious over the evil one. Amen.

Idol Treasures

Prayer Of Confession

Leader: O Lord, we have placed our faith in the things that do not satisfy.

People: We have gone after gods that are not gods at all.

Leader: We have accepted as truth that which is false.

People: We have sought our security in that which does not protect.

Leader: O God of the eternal, forgive us for laying up for ourselves treasures that will not last.

People: Not only forgive us, but help us to begin anew to pursue the true treasures of life,

Leader: The most precious of which is to know you. Amen.

Lost

Prayer Of Confession

Leader: God, our shepherd, we have strayed like lost sheep, wandering through life, far from home.

People: Often in our lives, we find ourselves in places where we ought not to be, trapped and unable to turn ourselves around.

Leader: At other times, out of fear, we huddle together,

People: Seeking safety rather than the joy of running free in the pastures you've given us.

Leader: Hear our lost cries. Come rescue us. Be our guide.

People: Startle us out of our comfortable safety, that we might run to the corners of the meadow,

Leader: Living as you would have us. Amen.

Reaching Out

Prayer Of Confession

Leader: People starving all around our world,

People: While we dress up and come to church.

Leader: Tears of sorrow, as our neighbors lose loved ones,

People: But we are busy doing church work.

Leader: Hungry souls searching for spiritual sustenance,

People: We wait, in the church, for them to come to us.

Leader: But they don't come, and we don't go. We should.

People: O Lord, forgive us for forgetting your command to go into all the world and make disciples.

Leader: Forgive us for developing a fortress mentality and hiding out in the church.

People: Teach us that the true church is people holding hands and reaching out to grasp the other hands,

Leader: The hands of the lost who need to be found; of the hungry who need to be fed; of the sorrowful who need to be comforted; of the chained who need to be freed;

People: Of the dying who need new life.

Leader: Lord, teach us! Amen.

Rebellion

Prayer Of Confession

Lord, we deny it, we pretend it isn't so, but the truth is that rebellion is part of our nature. Who among us hasn't rebelled against our leaders, our teachers, our parents? Who among us hasn't ignored you and your will for us? We have all sought, at one time or another, to be independent of you and your ways. Forgive our rebellious hearts. Help us to repent of our desire to rule in your place. Guide us home to your kingdom, and receive us, as you did the prodigal son, with arms open wide. Amen.

Seeds

Prayer Of Confession

Leader: An immense intellect, a seed.

People: A powerful voice, a seed.

Leader: A compassionate heart, a seed.

People: Nimble fingers, another seed.

Leader: A joyful spirit and an easy laugh, more seeds.

People: An amazing imagination, a basketful of seeds.

Leader: So many seeds you have given us, O Lord, we lament that we have not sown them.

People: We are afraid they will require too much work,

Leader: Take too much time.

People: Afraid they won't grow just right,

Leader: And people will think us foolish.

People: So we hold the seeds tight in our palms, denying them the chance to grow and bloom.

Leader: Forgive us, God of the seeds. And teach us to let go, to sow and let you grow

People: The mustard seeds within us into great trees where the world can find shade and fruit. Amen.

Self

Prayer Of Confession

Leader: If we are honest Lord, we must admit that we have lived too little for you and too much for ourselves.

People: We have pursued our comfort rather than your will.

Leader: We've trusted in ourselves, our abilities, our wealth, our ideas, rather than in you.

People: We've sought the safe rather than the faith that reaches out in love to the world.

Leader: We protected and hid our gifts of fear rather than letting them shine to tell the tale of your love for us.

People: Lord, forgive us. Strengthen our bonds to you that we might open our hearts, our minds, our hands, our selves without reservation,

Leader: Knowing that you will be with us always. Amen.

Self-Sufficiency

Prayer Of Confession

Leader: Lord, if there is one thing that is true of most of us, it is this: that we look for the answers everywhere but with you.

People: We try to be smart enough, dynamic enough, rich enough, brave enough to solve all of our problems.

Leader: But we discover that our brains, and bravery, and dollars, and dynamism aren't enough to quiet our troubled hearts.

People: Only you can do that. Only the power of your love can truly, and eternally, soothe our souls.

Leader: So help us to find the humility and the wisdom to stop trying to be "enough" ourselves, and to let you be enough for us.

People: Lord, teach us to surrender to your sufficiency, and to know the peace of that sweet surrender. Amen.

Shallow Lives

Prayer Of Confession

Leader: O Lord, you shine the radiant light of the living for us to follow,

People: But we prefer to hide in the dark, for fear of being seen.

Leader: You paint your creation with the colors of life,
People: But we prefer drab lives, for fear of being noticed.
Leader: You fill your world with variety, curiosities, adventures,
People: But we prefer to stay always home, for fear of risk or danger.
Leader: O Lord our God, forgive us for living so shallowly,
People: And fill us now with the courage to live fully, abundantly, faithfully. Amen.

Surrender
Prayer Of Confession

O Lord, our hearts say, "Follow the path of God's will. Trust in his promises." But our minds tell us, "Be careful! Stay safe. Hold on to the things the world gives." And we fight, our hearts and minds engaged in daily battle. Strengthen our hearts that we might find the will to give ourselves without reservation to you, following your sometimes scary way toward the prize of the Kingdom of Heaven. Amen.

Surrendered Lives
Prayer Of Confession

Leader: O God, we confess that we want to call you Lord,
People: But there are parts of our lives we haven't surrendered to you.
Leader: Too often we say, "You can come in here, Lord,
People: But stay out of this part of my life."
Leader: To be a Christian at church is okay,
People: But at work or at school is another matter.
Leader: To claim you, on Sunday, as Lord — YES!
People: But, on Monday, to make you Lord of our pocketbook, or our relationships, NO!
Leader: Lord who loves us always, help us!
People: Help us to turn our lives, our whole lives, over to you.
Leader: For in our surrender is our victory! Amen.

21

Unbelief

Prayer Of Confession

Leader: O Lord, maybe our greatest sin is selling you short.

People: We believe you love us, but not unconditionally.

Leader: We believe that you are ever-present,

People: But often feel as if you have abandoned us.

Leader: We believe in your power,

People: But not enough to trust you with our whole lives.

Leader: Help us to be sure,

People: So that we can fully accept your love, always know your presence, and come to trust you unconditionally. Amen.

Prayers Of Confession with Assurance Of Pardon

Blindness

Prayer Of Confession with Assurance Of Pardon

Leader: We confess today our blindness, O Lord.

People: We so often see only evil and darkness around us,

Leader: Hunger and sickness, hatred and violence, greed and selfishness.

People: We see your purposes being thwarted at every turn.

Leader: And wonder where you are, how long you will remain absent.

People: We begin to think you have abandoned us and our world.

Leader: We forget that even in the darkness, and despite the misery, you are still, miraculously, working your purposes.

People: Strengthen our sight that we might see through the darkness, behind the misery, around the self-centeredness,

Leader: And there discover the quiet, wonderful work of God that continues uninterrupted,

People: Keeping the light alive, and bringing new life where darkness and death presided before. Amen.

Brokenness And Hope

Prayer Of Confession with Assurance Of Pardon

Leader: O Father, we watch it happening all around us,

People: The crumbling of the nation.

Leader: Families are broken and torn apart.

People: Institutions betray the trust of the people.

Leader: Violence increases at every turn.

People: And we watch, horrified and dazed.

Leader: Forgive us when we allow our fear to paralyze us.

People: Forgive us for closing our eyes and hoping it will go away.

Leader: Give us the power and courage to give what we have to give to this dying people,

People: The love of the Lord of the living.

Leader: For your transforming love is our only true hope.

People: For there is no other name, no other power, by which we can be saved.

Leader: Let us rejoice in our salvation,

People: And spread the news! Amen!

Doubts

Prayer Of Confession with Assurance of Pardon

Leader: O Lord, we celebrate the new life you have given us.

People: We rejoice at justice won, at wounds healed, at courage given, at love shared.

Leader: Still though, there are times when doubt and cynicism overcome us.

People: We have given up on goodness, and mercy, and love.

Leader: Help us, as we struggle through the occasional fog in life, to know that though the fog obstructs our view,

People: The goodness, mercy, and love have not left us,

Leader: For they are of you,

People: And you never abandon us! Amen!

Failures
Prayer Of Confession with Assurance Of Pardon

Leader: So many times I have said to myself, "I will begin again, and this time I will get it right. I will pray more. I will read the Bible. I will be kinder, more disciplined, more of many things."

People: **And the new day dawns, and I begin, only to encounter obstacles, fail again, and despair once more.**

Leader: O God, forgive my foolish idea that I could ever get it totally right.

People: **Forgive my weakness that leads to so many failures.**

Leader: And forgive me the despair that comes because I fail to truly believe that you are a God who loves, and forgives,

People: **And gives me the power to get up when I fall, and begin again, over and over,**

Leader: Until the day I enter my perfection, and get it right, in your Kingdom. Amen.

Faithfulness
Prayer Of Confession with Assurance Of Pardon

Leader: Says the Psalmist, "I will meditate on your word day and night."

People: **We say, "Day and night? Get real!"**

Leader: The Psalmist says, "I will seek out your will, and focus my eyes on your ways."

People: **We say, "I'll say a quick prayer."**

Leader: David sings, "On the glorious splendor of your majesty, and on your wondrous works, I will think."

People: **We rarely think of God's glory, and too often forget the wonder of his work all around us.**

Leader: Jeremiah reminds us, "The patient love of the Lord is forever. His mercies never end, they are new every morning. Great is his faithfulness."

People: **And we say, "Thank you, Lord, for never giving up on us. Help us to turn to you to find truth and peace and joy." Amen.**

Fears

Prayer Of Confession with Assurance Of Pardon

Leader: Lord, the frustrating thing, the sad thing, is that even though we know you have set us free, still we live as if bound by heavy chains.

People: We live imprisoned by our fears.

Leader: We fear being unsuccessful, failures.

People: We fear financial insecurity.

Leader: We fear the uncertainty of tomorrow.

People: We fear for our children.

Leader: We fear illness and death.

People: Bound by the chains of fear, worry and anxiety, our precious freedom evaporates before our eyes.

Leader: Remind us, Lord, that we needn't live in chains. You have given us a pledge of eternal security which sets us free from every fear.

People: O God, forgive us our fears and tune our eyes, ears, and hearts to your truth that sets us free. Amen.

Freedom

Prayer Of Confession with Assurance Of Pardon

All: O God of boundless freedom, we carry our faith like a heavy burden: so many rules to follow, so many expectations to live up to, so many people to please, so many sins to avoid. The weight breaks our backs and wearies our spirits.

Leader: But your Word makes it clear that we have been set free, that the yoke of the law has been broken, the burden of sin lifted.

People: But still we submit. We live by law rather than love.

Leader: We judge ourselves and others with a terrible harshness.

People: Forgive our hard hearts, Lord. Soften us that we might see through eyes of love;

Leader: Hear with compassionate ears;

People: And live to bring glory, not to ourselves, but to you!

Leader: Let us live in the freedom of the Spirit, and according to the law of love. Amen.

Holiness
Prayer Of Confession with Assurance Of Pardon

Leader: O Holy God, you who are utterly different, we confess that we have sunk into sameness.

People: We have heard the call to be a people apart, but we have faltered and conformed to our world.

Leader: Few would say of us, "There's something different about them."

People: Few would say, "See how they love each other."

Leader: Few would think us odd for our generosity, or our joy, or our peace.

People: For we are like them, searching for happiness rather than holiness;

Leader: Trusting in ourselves rather than in you;

People: Pursuing personal prosperity rather than faithfully following the way of the cross.

Leader: Forgive us, Lord, when we get lost in the maddening crowd and go along where they lead.

People: Help us to hear, above the din, your still, small voice calling us out.

Leader: Let us never forget that we can come out to your side anytime we choose, and you will lead us along the way to the paradise of your presence. Amen.

In Search
Prayer Of Confession with Assurance Of Pardon

Leader: Lord, why is it we spend so much time trying to fit in?

People: Trying to be like everyone else?

Leader: Trying to find ourselves everywhere but in you?

People: We think maybe we'll find ourselves on the athletic field,

Leader: Or in the boardroom, or the bedroom,

People: Or some other room.

Leader: But all the while, we know, somewhere deep inside, that we will only truly find ourselves when we come home to you.

People: To you, the one who made us, and knows us, and loves us.

Leader: Turn our hearts toward home, our only true home.

People: Pull us to the bosom of the Father who made us,

Leader: To the arms of the Mother who cares for us,

People: To the warm, wonderful house of the Lord,

Leader: Where there is always a light lit for us. Amen.

Our Ways
Prayer Of Confession with Assurance Of Pardon

Leader: Dear Lord, you give us grace.

People: We give others judgment.

Leader: You selflessly give us your love.

People: We selfishly take for ourselves.

Leader: You show us the way of joy.

People: We follow our own ways, thinking we know better than you.

Leader: You give us abundant life.

People: We choose to live in safe, little hiding places, avoiding the risks of truly living.

Leader: Forgive our foolish ways.

People: Continue to grant us your grace.

Leader: Love us still, in spite of our straying ways.

People: And pull us ever closer to you that we might learn, one day, that you and you alone have the words and know the ways of life! Amen.

Out Of Tune
Prayer Of Confession with Assurance Of Pardon

Leader: Lord, for keeping the beautiful music of the gospel to ourselves,

People: We ask forgiveness.

Leader: For turning from the music ourselves and listening instead to the strains of selfishness,

People: We beg your pardon.

Leader: For trying to dance to both your music and the world's,

People: We seek acquittal,

27

Leader: And pray that you will grant us the enormous courage we need to take the risk of dancing to your good news band,

People: Rather than the tune of sin to which the world dances.

Leader: We thank you that you are a God who continues, always, to play on,

People: And who dances with us whenever we finally decide to become your partner.

Leader: Praise God, the Lord of the Dance!

People: Amen!

Prayer

Prayer Of Confession

Leader: O Lord, teach us to pray. We don't know how.

People: It seems a dry, lifeless, empty exercise to us. We don't have time. We don't know how. We don't understand. Lord, teach us to pray.

Leader: Teach us to clear the clutter and clatter from our lives that we might hear your still, small voice, the voice that whispers to us the secrets of life, the voice that guides us in hidden paths of peace, and righteousness, and love, and joy.

People: O Lord, teach us to pray! Amen!

Assurance Of Pardon

Leader: As a mother loves her children, so God loves us.

People: His love wipes our tears, calms our fears, builds our courage, guides our way, forgives our sins, makes us whole.

Leader: But the Father's motherly, life-giving love cannot reach us and heal us and fill us if we turn from him.

People: We are forgiven! We are loved!

Leader: Let us turn to him and receive his love. Amen.

Sin

Prayer Of Confession with Assurance Of Pardon

Leader: Let's just make an honest confession today.

People: Lord, we have sinned!

Leader: Sometimes we try to pretend we haven't,

People: Or we rationalize that others do it more than we

Leader: But the bald-faced truth is ...

People: That we have sinned.

Leader: All of us, every single one, all the time ...

People: We do or say or think judgmental things.

Leader: We fail to respond to an obvious need.

People: We want what is not ours.

Leader: The list is long and it hardly matters what is on it. All that matters is that we have sinned,

People: And that you, in your great mercy, will forgive each of us for every sin if we turn to you,

Leader: Claim Jesus as Savior, and make him Lord of our lives. Let us accept this good news and make it our own. Amen.

Spiritual Battle

Prayer Of Confession

Leader: In the battle for the soul of the world we are God's soldiers,

People: The first wave of the invasion force storming the beaches of evil.

Leader: But, Lord, we must confess that too often we ignore your orders. We refuse to engage in the battle. We are found AWOL as the battle unfolds.

People: Too often we've forgotten why we are here.

Leader: We've left the battle to others.

People: Sometimes we've even joined the enemy,

Leader: Unrepentingly sinning, turning our backs on injustice, neglecting our neighbors.

People: Accept now our repentance, Lord.

Leader: Forgive our failures, and help us once again to take our place on the front lines of the great battle for the soul of the world.

Assurance Of Pardon

Leader: Hear now this good news. Our request has been heard. Forgiveness is granted and our Lord has promised all who take part in the battle that nothing, not angels or demons, not the present or the future, not life or death, nothing in all creation can separate us from his love.

People: **Praise the Lord! Praise his holy name! Amen!**

Assurance Of Pardon

Forgiveness
Assurance Of Pardon

Leader: And here is the message which we carry as ambassadors of the gospel of good news. We have been saved from sin and death by the grace of God whose Son of love gave his life for our freedom. Take the news into all the land, "No death can hold any who are in Christ."

People: **Praise God for his forgiveness.**
Praise God for his victory. Amen.

Prayers For Illumination

Bread Of Life
Prayer For Illumination

Dear heavenly Father, on your Word we feed each week. It is to us like manna from heaven, a gift, a bit of grace, nourishment for our weary souls. Become to us once more this morning the Bread of Life. Feed us as we read, listen, sing, pray, and commune together around your table. Amen!

Breath Of Life
Prayer For Illumination

O God whose breath is life, send out to our weary hearts and tired spirits these words of yours on the wings of that breath. Breathe into us the new life of your Word. Amen.

Create Anew
Prayer For Illumination
Eternal God, Creator of every living thing, create in us now clear heads and clean hearts for the hearing of this Word. Amen.

Ears To Hear
Prayer For Illumination
"For those who have ears to hear," said Jesus, "let them hear." Dear Lord, give us such ears this morning that we might hear the particular word you have for each one of us. Pour out your blessing on those who sing and preach, that they might be instruments of your message. Amen.

Light For The Path
Prayer For Illumination
O Lord, our lives often get so bogged down in a hailstorm of little things that we can't see the path of abundant life that you have mapped out for us. May your Word today be a sparkling ray of light, grabbing our attention, that we might lift up our heads and see your way again. Amen.

Living Word
Prayer For Illumination
To hear your Word is one thing, O Lord, to live it quite another. Strengthen us, enliven us, empower us, for the living of your Word and will. Amen.

Speak Your Word
Prayer For Illumination
O Speaker of the Word, speak into our cluttered minds a word of clarity. Speak into our fragmented hearts a word of wholeness. Speak into our misguided wills a word of truth. Amen.

Teach And Guide

Prayer For Illumination

Lord, as a mother reads stories and a father tells tales to their children, so you give us the scripture to teach and guide us. Help us listen today, as wide-eyed children, to the good news story of your Word. Amen.

Voice Of God

Prayer For Illumination

Leader: Our Father, the voices that tell us we are worthless, useless, helpless, and hopeless we hear loud and clear.

People: Let our hearts hear another voice this morning.

Leader: Let us hear your sweet voice whispering to us the truth,

People: That we are your beloved children,

Leader: That there is purpose in life,

People: That you are our help,

Leader: That our hope is sure,

People: For you are the almighty God of all creation.

Leader: Let us hear the voice of God. Amen.

Chapter 2

General Liturgies Collections

Collections I
(Call To Worship, Prayer Of Confession, Prayer For Illumination)

Beauty Within
Call To Worship
Leader: It is a treasure trove of possibilities:
An incredible collection of talents,
A wonderland of beauty and splendor,
A diamond in the rough, waiting to sparkle.

People: What is it? What is it you speak of?

Leader: Of you! I speak of you.

People: Me? That doesn't sound much like me.

Leader: That's only because you don't see with the eyes of God. He sees through you, inside you. He sees what he filled you with when he made you.

People: It's a nice feeling.

Leader: What is?

People: The feeling that comes from knowing God sees the sparkle and beauty in me.

Leader: It *is* a good feeling. Let's hold on to it. Let's celebrate it this morning, the image of God in us. Let's remember that we are:

People: Treasure troves of possibilities,

Leader: Incredible collections of talent,

People: Wonderlands of beauty and splendor,

Leader: Diamonds in the rough, waiting to sparkle.

People: Amen.

Leader: Let's worship our God, the virtuoso of creators.

Prayer Of Confession
Leader: You know, I've been thinking about this diamond in the rough thing. When I look at myself, I wonder if I'm ever going to get polished up.

People: I know the feeling.

Leader: And sometimes you can't see the beauty for the sin in me.

People: I know that feeling, too!

Leader: And I know I've let my Maker down, more times than I can count, when it comes to sharing my gifts and talents.

People: Haven't we all?

Leader: Let us pray.

Prayer For Illumination

Dear Lord, we rejoice that you have filled us with things beautiful and wonderful, but we grieve that we have hidden, covered up, ignored, and hoarded what you've given us. Forgive us. Remind us that no matter how deeply we bury it, the beauty is always there waiting to be uncovered and shared with the world. Help us to uncover what you have placed in each of us. Amen.

Living Water

Call To Worship

Leader: He, a weary traveler, sat down for a rest.

People: She came to the well to draw water for the day.

Leader: He said, "Give me a drink."

People: She was surprised. "How is it that you, a Jew, ask me, a Samaritan woman, for a drink?"

Leader: For Jews hated Samaritans, but not this Jew.
He said, "If you only knew who I am, you would ask me for living water."

People: But he had nothing with which to draw water. "Where do you get this water from, sir?"

Leader: "And wonderful water it is. For whoever drinks of it shall never again thirst."

People: "O give me this water that I may not thirst."

Leader: And they talked on until she began to realize that she *was* drinking in his water of life, his wisdom, his truth, his self.

People: Let us, too, drink at his well.

Leader: Let us worship God. Amen.

Prayer Of Confession

Leader: O Lord, some of us, this week, hurt someone we love, with our words or lack of concern.

People: Some of us deceived another for our own gain.

Leader: Some behaved irresponsibly, and now regret our actions.

People: Some allowed our greed, or selfishness, to rule our hearts.

Leader: Some of us hated ourselves for not measuring up.

People: But this is the way it is in the kingdom of the human race.

Leader: The kingdom of imperfection, where everyone falls short in one way or another.

People: Remind us, Lord, of your bountiful forgiveness.

Leader: Help us to look past the imperfections in ourselves and others, to see the core of beauty that you've placed in each of us,

People: And to live in joyful anticipation of the day of our perfection. Amen.

Prayer For Illumination

God of life, give us the water that only you can give: water from the stormy seas of truth to set us free; from the raging rivers of life to revitalize us; from the serene streams of peace to calm our anxious souls. Amen.

Oneness In Christ

Call To Worship

Leader: Out of the world, from the ends of the earth, we come to this place each Sunday.

People: From places of success and failure;

Leader: From high peaks of joy, and deep, dark valleys of anguish;

People: From places where the sunrise of new life has just dawned;

Leader: To places where the sun is setting and life is nearing its end.

People: From all these places and more,

Leader: From diversity that boggles the mind,

People: We come to the one place where we are one —

Leader: To the church! Where we are all of the same baptism, same faith, same Lord.

People: So let us celebrate our God-given differences,

Leader: And rejoice in our hard-won oneness in Christ Jesus, the Lord of all.

People: Amen.

Prayer Of Confession

Leader: Out with the old and in with the new! That's what they say, isn't it?

People: Yeah, I guess so.

Leader: But you don't seem very enthusiastic about it.

People: Well, I like the old.

Leader: Really? But the new seems so much better to me. Why do you like the old?

People: I guess I'm just comfortable with it. And why do you like the new?

Leader: I love change. It suits my personality. I'm comfortable with it.

People: Ahh, there's that word again, comfortable.

Leader: Do you suppose maybe we spend too much time looking for comfort and too little time seeking out God's will?

People: I'm sorry to say you're probably right.

Leader: Maybe we should ask God to help us be less concerned with our own comfort and more concerned with his will.

People: Let's pray.

Prayer For Illumination

Dear Lord, help us to see through our own selfish desires. Help us to give up our longing to be comfortable. Help us to be a people with a passion for love and justice, a people after your heart, a people of God. Amen.

Collections II
(Call To Worship, Prayer Of Confession with Assurance Of Pardon)

Burdens Lifted

Call To Worship

Leader: O Lord, to come here each week and place our lives in your hands,

People: This is a great blessing.

Leader: To lay down our burdens for just a few moments at your feet,

People: This is a sweet refreshment.

Leader: To free our spirits and let them soar as you intend them to,

People: This is deep joy.

Leader: O Lord, we come now to do these things,

People: And to worship you for making them possible.

Leader: Let us worship our God!!

People: Amen!

Prayer Of Confession

Dear Father, many of us come here today bent over from the burdens of life in our fallen world. Sorrows surround us. Our sin suffocates us. Self-hatred strangles our joy. Remind us in this time, in this moment, in the depths of our hearts, that you are the burden-lifter. So lift all of the burdens that our sin has heaped upon us, and give us the abundant life Jesus promised us. Amen.

Assurance Of Pardon

Leader: He has promised us that all the burdens can be lifted from the shoulders of those who take up their crosses and follow where he leads.

People: Let us follow where he leads.

Leader: And we will know the peace that cannot be fully understood.

People: We will know the Sabbath rest of Yahweh.

Leader: Praise the Lord for his rest!

People: Praise the Lord! Amen!

Come To Me

Call To Worship

Leader: Jesus said, "Come to me, all who labor and are heavy laden, and I will give you rest.

People: Take my yoke upon you, and learn from me; for I am gentle and lowly in heart, and you will find rest for your souls.

Leader: For my yoke is easy, and my burden is light."

People: We have come with burdens.

Leader: Lay them down.

People: We have come heavy-laden with sorrows and concerns.

Leader: Let them go, for we have come into the house of the One who gives rest and renews life!

People: Let us worship him!

Prayer Of Confession with Assurance of Pardon

Leader: Lord, we come not to confess any great sin this morning, but to confess our shortsightedness.

People: We see the problems and concerns of today.

Leader: We feel the burdens and stresses of life.

People: We hear the cries and sorrows that surround us.

Leader: Help us, Lord, to get a longer view.

People: Help us to see the glorious, beautiful light at the end of this darkness in which we walk.

Leader: For with you, Lord, the darkness never defeats the light.

People: With you there are new mercies every morning.

Leader: With you there is only victory!

People: Transform us into conquerors, Lord, that we might defeat the darkness of this world. Amen.

Faith Journey

Call To Worship

Leader: Abram and Sarai packed up their bags, left their homes, and journeyed to Canaan, at the Lord's call: Journeying against the grain.

People: We celebrate their faith today!

Leader: Abraham led his son Isaac up Mount Moriah to give him to the Lord: Climbing against the grain.

People: We are awed by such trust in you, Yahweh.

Leader: Esther approached the king, risking her life for her people: Standing tall against the grain.

People: We admire her courageous faith.

Leader: Daniel prayed when it was against the law, refused to recant even as he faced a den of hungry lions: Living against the grain.

People: We long to have a faith such as his.

Leader: We live in a world that worships the material, celebrates the self, and majors in life's minor things.

People: Let us follow in the faithful footsteps of our forebears — Abraham and Sarah, Esther and Daniel, Peter and Paul — even though they lead us against the grain of a world gone astray.

Leader: And let's begin by opening our hearts and minds to the One who was the source of their faith, their strength, their lives, our God, Yahweh!

People: Amen!

Prayer Of Confession with Assurance Of Pardon

Leader: Lord, we are very good at believing in you when it is convenient.

People: We trumpet our faith, pledge our allegiance, until you ask something difficult of us.

Leader: Then we retreat. We forget. We ignore.

People: When you ask us to give up some cherished old habit, we grip tighter.

Leader: When you call us to patiently wait, we complain.

People: When you point to the unlovable and tell us to love them, we turn our backs.

Leader: Lord, forgive us our deep selfishness.

People: Forgive us for trying to tell you how things ought to be.

Leader: Forgive us for going along, instead of swimming against, the current of a culture that seeks all the wrong things.

41

People: We ask your help to turn into the tide and swim as hard as we can when you call us to do so.

Leader: And we praise you that each time we fail, each time we float along, you do forgive us. Keep calling us, Lord, and keep forgiving us our failings.

People: For we ask it in Jesus' name. Amen.

The Promise

Call To Worship

Leader: The Promise was made to Abraham and Sarah.

People: And they lived for the promise all the days of their lives,

Leader: Even though the fullness of the promise was never theirs to taste.

People: The Promise was made to Isaac,

Leader: Who lived in anticipation of its fulfillment all his years,

People: Even as he lay bound to an altar with a knife poised above his breast.

Leader: The Promise was made to Moses,

People: Who was faithful to it even as he lay dying on the doorstep to the Promised Land.

Leader: The Promise was made to Mary and twelve of the most ordinary men on earth.

People: And they gave themselves to it all the way to their own martyrdom.

Leader: And the Promise has been made to us,

People: The Promise that God will love us, and lead us to a glorious land where we will be granted new and everlasting leases on life.

Leader: And its taste is sweet in the mouths of those whose hearts are open and whose feet are firmly planted on the way of God.

People: This is a Promise to celebrate!

Leader: Let us worship God!

Prayer Of Confession with Assurance Of Pardon

You promise, Lord, but we don't believe. We say we do. We want to, but we can't get past the doubts the world plants in our heads. We can't quite believe that you are real; that you love us unconditionally; that eternal life awaits us. O Lord, help our unbelief. Plant the Promise deep in our hearts where the blight of doubt cannot reach it. And make us whole, as only you can. Amen.

The Way

Call To Worship

Leader: One day a father sent his child on a journey through the woods.

People: O, how the child was afraid.

Leader: But the father said, "I have carved out a path for you to follow. If you stay on the road all the way, you will never get lost or be in danger."

People: And the child was relieved that the father had made a way through the frightening woods.

Leader: Let's rejoice, for the Father has made us a way through the woods,

**People: A way that is perfect, a way that is sure,
A way that is right, a way that is pure.**

Leader: Let us worship the God of the Way.

Prayer Of Confession

Leader: But it seems it always happens that this child, who fully intends to stay on the way, strays.

People: Gee, that path looks much more interesting than my father's. I'd really like to see those flowers. Maybe I'll go that way.

Leader: And before the child goes far from his father's way, he, or maybe she, is lost.

People: O, it's so dark in here. I can't see. Which way is out? Where am I? Who am I? Help me! Someone help me! I'm lost.

Leader: When will we learn, Dear Father, that your way is the only way?

People: Teach us to walk your way. Amen.

Assurance Of Pardon

Leader: Yes, the Father teaches us his way, but what of the already lost child?

People: **And the child who gets lost many times on the way, what of him?**

Leader: Well, despite his disobedience, his Father will come and find him, and set him on the road again, if only the child will ask.

People: **O Father, give us the discipline to stay on your way, and come find each child who has strayed and return them to the way. Amen.**

Water of Life

Call To Worship

Leader: Hey, are you thirsty this morning?

People: **Some of us come as dry as bones.**

Leader: Then come to the well like the woman of Samaria,

People: **Who came to fill her bucket,**

Leader: And had her heart filled instead,

People: **With a never-ending river of living waters.**

Leader: Come to the well, and drink long the waters of the love of God,

People: **For these are the only waters that truly satisfy the soul thirst that plagues us.**

Leader: Come, let us go to the well and drink.

People: **Amen.**

Prayer Of Confession with Assurance Of Pardon

Leader: O Lord, some of us are wondering lately where you are.

People: **We can't see you, or feel your presence, or hear your voice anymore. Where have you gone?**

Leader: But we know, in that place inside us where the voice of truth still speaks, we know that you have gone nowhere.

People: **We know that it is we who have turned our backs and walked away from you.**

Leader: Help us all, today, to feel deeply how badly we need you.

People: **Make it a raging fire in our souls,**

Leader: That burns us up, until we return to you.

People: **For it is only in you that we will find peace. Amen.**

Collections III
(Call To Worship, Prayer Of Confession)

A New Day
Call To Worship

Leader: Let us rejoice, for morning has dawned.
A new day has been born,
and we are alive to enjoy it!

People: **We celebrate the beauty of God's creation**
and the wonder of the human family.

Leader: We remember those whose love and sacrifice
has shaped our lives.

People: **We hope and work for a future**
where justice flourishes and love rules.

Leader: We hope and work for the Kingdom of God
to come on earth as it is in Heaven.

People: **O God, bless us so that what we do in this time**
sows seeds of joy, gratitude, and hope. Amen.

Prayer Of Confession

Leader: We go to bed at night, heads swirling with "to do's"; things
that need to be done, worries, problems to solve, all man-
ner of concerns.

People: **We lie awake, spinning schemes to save, to solve, to**
win, to get ahead.

Leader: And sleep is sometimes an elusive stranger even though
your scriptures promise that you give your loved ones
sleep.

People: **We confess, O Lord, that we can't stop thinking that**
it is all up to us. We can't lay down our burdens at
your feet because we do not yet trust you.

Leader: Give us that peace that soothes and calms but is beyond our understanding.

People: **And let us lie down and rise up with this peace as our constant companion. We pray in the name of our Lord Jesus Christ. Amen.**

Fear Of The Lord

Call To Worship

Leader: The beginning of wisdom is the fear of the Lord.

People: **We come today, O Lord, awed at your grandeur;**

Leader: Overwhelmed at your majesty;

People: **Grateful for your grace;**

Leader: Smitten by your love.

People: **Grant us today the beginnings of wisdom.**

Leader: Let us worship God. Amen.

Prayer Of Confession

Leader: Grand and glorious God, we are uncomfortable with the idea of fearing you.

People: **We want to modify the idea.**

Leader: We want to say, "respect," or "revere," but not fear.

People: **We are uncomfortable with a God we must fear.**

Leader: Teach us, Lord, that you are to be feared for you are the almighty God of the universe.

People: **At your word the world came into being.**

Leader: At your touch the seas parted before Israel.

People: **At your command the dead have been restored to life.**

Leader: Your power is truly awesome.

People: **And though we know you are a God of love,**

Leader: Though we know you love us,

People: **Still we must "fear" you.**

Leader: Forgive us for trying to cut you down to a size we can be comfortable with.

People: **Make us wise by revealing to us just how fearful, how awesome, you are. Amen.**

Friends

Call To Worship

Leader: Adam was lonely in paradise,

People: So the Lord gave him Eve.

Leader: And they rejoiced,

People: Celebrating the goodness of togetherness.

Leader: David and Jonathan were brothers of the heart;

People: Friends who knew their love was forever.

Leader: In our days of gladness, God gives us friends

People: To share and multiply our happiness.

Leader: On the days when we carry heavy burdens, our brothers and sisters

People: Lend their shoulders and help lift the burden.

Leader: Many gifts we've been given, but the gift of friends,

People: This gift is among the greatest.

Leader: Let us praise God, who loves us through our friends.

People: Alleluia! Amen!

Prayer Of Confession

Leader: Our confession this morning is very specific, Lord: too many times we have failed our friends.

People: We have allowed them to struggle through hardships without our help.

Leader: We have ignored them for long stretches of time.

People: We have turned a deaf ear to their attempts to speak the truth to us in love.

Leader: We have even betrayed them behind their backs with angry words.

People: And worst of all, we have tried to convince ourselves that we have no need of friends.

Leader: Lord, remind us that without friends of faith, we cannot stand firm in our faith,

People: That we need each other,

Leader: And we are called to love each other as you have loved us.

People: For in this, the world will know we are Christians.

Leader: And in this, you will be glorified. Amen.

God

Call To Worship

Leader: Imagine, he is the Creator and Ruler of all things,

People: Infinite and eternal God,

Leader: Omnipotent and awesome King,

People: Perfect in power and in knowledge,

Leader: Terrible, but just, Judge,

People: Holy, other, majestic, beyond us.

Leader: But, imagine too, he is love!

People: Pure, unconditional, gracious love,

Leader: A father, a mother, a lover of all,

People: Relational, and real, and with us always.

Leader: He is our God! Let us celebrate his power and give thanks for his love as we worship him together.

People: Amen!

Leader: Amen!

Prayer Of Confession

Leader: We live as if God exists for us, as if his only purpose is to make us happy.

People: We put our fulfillment and satisfaction at the center of the universe.

Leader: Making it not only our highest priority, but God's as well.

People: Lord, forgive us for falling into the self-centered thinking that the world presses on us.

Leader: Convince us that it is in giving up our freedom that we become free, it is in losing our lives that we find life.

People: Convince us that only by following you and your way of selflessness do we find real fulfillment. Amen.

God Reigns

Call To Worship

Leader: Our God reigns!

People: In places high and low.

Leader: Our God reigns.

People: Over earth and wind and fire,

48

Leader: Over kings and queens and governments,

People: Over the principalities and powers we cannot see,

Leader: Over the hearts of men and women who submit to his loving, gracious rule.

People: May we have such hearts!

Leader: Let us praise our God who reigns!

Prayer Of Confession

Leader: We are sorry to say, Lord, that the story of Adam and Eve is our story.

People: We have tried our best to elbow you out of our lives and run things ourselves.

Leader: We wish to be in control and on top of things,

People: But you have made it clear to us that when we claim your throne, things go badly for us.

Leader: We fight, and hate, and separate ourselves from each other.

People: We lie, and steal, and sink into the sands of guilt.

Leader: We medicate, and escape from life, and feel dead and empty.

People: Father, bring us to a place in our lives where we are so broken that we, like the prodigal son, realize that we need to return to you.

Leader: And place you properly on the throne of our lives that it may be well with us.

People: We confess our need for you, and praise you for your loving reception of us. Amen!

God Speaks

Call To Worship

Leader: O Lord, there is no pretending with you.

People: We can come here with our nice clothes and our painted-on smiles, but you see past them.

Leader: You see that we are sad, or lonely, or anxious, or angry, or weak.

People: You see that all is not well with us.

Leader: So speak to the person behind our pretense this morning.

People: Speak to the real us.

Leader: Speak to us the words we need to hear.

People: Speak peace to the anxious and fearful.

Leader: Speak hope to the sad and fearful.

People: Speak comfort to the lonely and burdened.

Leader: Speak freedom to the bound and strength to the weak.

People: Lord, we have come to hear you. Speak to us now.

Prayer Of Confession

Leader: We know, Lord, most of the time the problem is not your lack of speaking to us, but our lack of listening to you.

People: Forgive us our many distractions.

Leader: Forgive us for turning attention to everything and everyone but you.

People: Forgive us for ignoring what we know you have said to us already.

Leader: And help us to hear the Word that never stops seeking out our hearts, that it might rest and nest there,

People: And grow into a peace that can't be shattered.

Leader: Amen.

House Of God

Call To Worship

Leader: Week after week, month after month, year after year, we return to this place;

People: The house of the Lord God.

Leader: We come here to sing, to praise, to pray;

People: To rest in the warm bosom of our faith family;

Leader: To hear, to be reminded, to be challenged;

People: To unburden ourselves and to drink long at the well of God's refreshing presence.

Leader: Ultimately though, we come here because we belong here,

People: For we are the people of God.

Leader: We are the ones of his own choosing.

People: And this is home, our Father's place.

Leader: Welcome home.

People: Glad to be here.

Leader: Let us worship our Father. Amen.

Prayer Of Confession

Leader: Lord, we do often think of this place as your home, and in some ways it is, but we know that you do not live here.

People: We know that your true home is the hearts of those who love you.

Leader: So many times we forget that.

People: We think that six days a week we are alone against the world.

Leader: So we run away when we ought to stand tall; we turn our backs on the young man who's being tormented by our friends; we ignore the potbellied babies of Rwanda; we surrender to the worldly attitudes of materialism and secularism.

People: O Lord, remind us this morning that when we leave this safe haven, you go with us.

Leader: And each time we face the difficult challenge of living as a Christian in this world, remind us that your strength resides in us,

People: That we might be beacons of light in the world's darkness. Amen.

Limiting God

Call To Worship

Leader: Do you think God is a man or a woman?

People: I don't know. But I've always thought of him as a father.

Leader: Me, too. I love the image of a gentle, loving Father God.

People: So he must be a man.

Leader: I don't think so. The Bible also speaks of him as a Mother who nurtures her children.

People: So God is a woman! Or both!

Leader: Let's just say, God is God. And let us worship the gentle Father who loves us,

People: And the warm Mother who cares for us.

Leader: Let us worship our God.

Prayer Of Confession

Leader: Lord, we think of you so often in ways that limit you.

People: We make you into a sweet mother who has no backbone and can be bent to our desires.

Leader: Or an awesome but angry Father who is far away and to be dreaded.

People: Or the one who takes our side against our enemies.

Leader: Or the dear old friend we visit on Sunday mornings, but ignore the rest of the week.

People: Or something else that limits you.

Leader: But you are God! Whose ways and thoughts are so much higher than ours,

People: Who we can love, and worship, and follow,

Leader: But whom we can never fully grasp, for even in all our glory as your creatures, we are far too small to understand your fullness.

People: Grant us humility to remember who we are. Amen.

Lord God Almighty

Call To Worship

Leader: Holy, holy, holy are you, the Lord God Almighty.

People: Heaven and earth are full of your glory.

Leader: Everywhere we turn we are reminded of your power,

People: For you light the day with the sun, and the night with the moon.

Leader: You paint the seas and skies with curious and beautiful creatures.

People: You fill the fields with flowers and foods.

Leader: You breathe life into your children's bodies and spirits.

People: And conquer death for us with your love.

Leader: You are an awesome God!

People: And, like Isaiah before us, we bow down before you!

Leader: Let us worship GOD!

Prayer Of Confession

Leader: Almighty and Everlasting Lord, forgive our attempts to fit you into our ways of thinking.

People: Forgive us for demanding that you operate according to our rules,

Leader: And for rejecting you when you don't.

People: You are a big God, bigger than we can imagine.

Leader: Break through our self-centered thinking and help us understand how gloriously great you are,

People: That we might be humbled like Job, freed from our need to control all things,

Leader: And comforted by the knowledge that you are still in charge, working out all things for the good of those who love you. Amen.

Redeeming Love

Call To Worship

Leader: Praise God for he has done glorious things!

People: He has lifted our lives from the snarl of sin and the darkness of death and freed us for new life!

Leader: Praise God for he works in our lives today!

People: To make us more and more into the image and likeness of our Lord Jesus Christ.

Leader: Praise God for he will work tomorrow!

People: To restore, in this world, the paradise lost long ago through sin.

Leader: Yahweh is the God of yesterday, today, and tomorrow.

People: Let us worship the awesome God of the universe.

Prayer Of Confession

Leader: O Lord, we know that you love all people, and call us to do the same,

People: But we confess how hard it is for us to love some people.

Leader: There are people whose ideas are so different from ours that we must hate them.

People: And people who beliefs don't sit well with us, so we reject them.

Leader: And people whose skin color is different, so we fear them.

People: And people who are so disagreeable that we cannot seem to help but dislike them.
Leader: But you have shown us that in you there is oneness.
People: In you there is something that holds us together that transcends race, belief, ideas, even temperament.
Leader: In you there is LOVE!
People: Forgive us the dislike and hatred that divides us, Lord,
Leader: And teach us all to love as you do. Amen.

Collections IV
(Prayer Of Confession, Prayer For Illumination)

Hurting World
Prayer Of Confession
Leader: Starving millions in Somalia.
People: It hurts too much to look, Lord.
Leader: Thousands wasting away of AIDS.
People: We'd like to think it's all their own fault, because we don't know what to do about it.
Leader: Crack babies and inner cities like war zones.
People: They scare us so we stay away.
Leader: Friends with no health care.
People: We throw up our hands in disgust.
Leader: Poverty, hunger, sickness, war. Problems that paralyze us, overwhelm us.
People: Dear God, forgive us our excuses and rationalizations that keep us from acting and validate our selfishness. Move us to reach out, to do what we can with our time and our money to help our brothers and sisters everywhere. Amen.

Prayer For Illumination
May you, O God, who sees the outcast on her knees, and the dying in his bed, and the grief-stricken with her tears, and the hungry at his empty table, help us to see as you see, and do as you would have us do. Amen.

Misplaced Trust

Prayer Of Confession

Leader: Holiest Father, we confess that we have turned away from you, and forgotten that you are our hope and peace.

People: We have placed our trust in our business, our organizations, our politics, and our incomes.

Leader: We trust the things that cannot satisfy the longings of the heart, or the yearnings of the spirit.

People: Forgive us our misplaced trust, our lack of faith in you and your love for us.

Leader: Help us once again to know that you are the only Father in whom is found true life, and that none of these things can be trusted to love us, guide us, heal us, make us whole.

People: Turn our hearts once again toward you, O Lord. Amen!

Prayer For Illumination

O Lord, there is so much in our world that entices us away from you, so much to desire, to crave, to be greedy about. But we want to grow to maturity, to see past the superficial to the deep, to the true, to the things that satisfy the soul. Give us such sight today. Amen.

Seek Godliness

Prayer Of Confession

Leader: Blessed are the poor in spirit, says the Lord.

People: But the world says, and we long, to be rich.

Leader: Blessed are the meek.

People: But we want to be strong and powerful.

Leader: Unless you become as children ...

People: But children are small, weak, insignificant.

Leader: Those who want to be great must be the servants of all.

People: But the great are the ones who are served.

Leader: The first shall be last, and the last first.

People: O Lord, we confess that we do not accept, we don't even understand your teaching about humility.

Leader: We have utterly misunderstood greatness.

People: Change our hearts, dear Jesus, that instead of worldly greatness we might seek godly greatness.

Leader: Instead of fame,

People: Faithfulness!

Leader: In place of money,

People: The incomparable riches of grace!

Leader: Rather than power,

People: The fullness of love!

Leader: Make us over, Lord, in your beautiful image.

People: Amen!

Prayer For Illumination

Lord, we seek life in many places. We look to the health spa, to the beauty parlor, to the liquor store, the stock market, and many other places. But there is one place where true life is to be found, in you. Free us to come now to the scriptures, and hear your life-giving words, and live! Amen.

True Riches

Prayer Of Confession

O God, we confess we have become rich by our greed. We do not know how to become rich by caring, loving and helping others. O God, heal our greediness and teach us your ways that lead to true riches!

Prayer For Illumination

Open our hearts to hear the message of the true riches. Make us see the beauty of the riches of life. Have love and happiness fill our hearts, not the love of money. Amen.

Vision

Prayer Of Confession

Leader: O Lord, it is true. Our vision of the future is filled with cars and houses and portfolios and titles;

People: But you are often nowhere to be found.

Leader: We accept things as they are and operate as those before us have.

People: **Your call, though, is to create a new future, a future of hope and peace and loveliness.**

Leader: Capture our hearts, dear Lord, that we might catch your vision for the future,

People: **And play a part in bringing it to pass. Amen.**

Prayer For Illumination

Leader: O God, be to us now a burning bush,

People: **That we might sense your glory in the world around us,**

Leader: That we might feel the warmth of your flame,

People: **That we might ourselves be kindled by the spirit**

Leader: And shine as bright lights to the world. Amen.

Chapter 3

Advent Liturgies

Collections
(Call To Worship, Prayer Of Confession)

A Child Is Born
Call To Worship

Leader: Day after day our world seems to grow darker.

People: As nation rises against nation and people against people,

Leader: As neighbors turn on one another and violence increases,

People: As hunger rampages through the earth,

Leader: And poverty and pestilence conquer many,

People: As morals decay and families crumble, the darkness deepens.

Leader: But in the midst, God's prophet speaks,

People: "The people who walked in darkness have seen a great light;

Leader: Those who dwelt in a land of deep darkness, on them has light shined.

People: For the Lord shall increase our joy; he will break the yoke of our burden,

Leader: And every boot of the tramping warrior in battle tumult and every garment rolled in blood will be burned as fuel for the fire.

People: For to us a child is born, to us a son is given;

Leader: And the government will be upon his shoulder, and his name will be called 'Wonderful Counselor, Mighty God, Everlasting Father, Prince of Peace.'

People: Of the increase of his government and of peace there will be no end,

Leader: And his will be a kingdom that upholds justice and righteousness for evermore." Amen.

Prayer Of Confession

Leader: It always comes to this, every year at this time, the question comes, "Who is this child lying in the manger?"

People: The question is, as Jesus asked his disciples, "Who do we say that he is?"

Leader: And our answers are many.

People: Some say he is the greatest teacher who ever lived.

Leader: Others say he is a grand moral example.

People: Some think of him as a brave prophet who spoke against injustice and died for his principles.

Leader: But we say, in the church, that he is the way and the truth and the life.

People: We say that the way home to paradise is through his death.

Leader: We say that he reveals the truth of God's deep love for us.

People: We say that in him, and only in him, is the fullness of life.

Leader: We say, he is God's Son, our Savior, and our Lord. Let us follow him.

People: Let us follow. Amen.

Angels

Call To Worship

Leader: To quiet men, out in a field,

People: Came an angel in all his frightening glory.

Leader: "Be not afraid, for behold, I bring you good news of a great joy."

People: And they were filled with fear as they heard him proclaim,

Leader: "For to you is born this day, in the city of David, a Savior, who is Christ the Lord."

People: And when the angels had left them, they went to Bethlehem to see this amazing thing,

Leader: Finding, as they had been told, a babe lying in a manger, wrapped in swaddling clothes.

People: And they returned home rejoicing and praising God for all they had seen.

Leader: The angel still announces each Christmas, "Be not afraid, for behold, I bring you good news."

People: But will we listen? Will we hear?

Leader: "For to you there has been born, in your heart, a Savior, who is Christ the Lord."

People: Let us find him there, and rejoice! Amen!

Prayer Of Confession

Leader: Dear Father, your angels abound around us,

People: But somehow their glory escapes our eyes, and their songs slip into the background.

Leader: There is good news,

People: But we hear only the bad.

Leader: There is great joy,

People: But we see only pain.

Leader: There is powerful love,

People: But we rarely allow it to touch us.

Leader: Turn our eyes and ears upward, O Lord,

People: And our hearts outward,

Leader: That we might see the glory of the angels,

People: Hear their joyous song,

Leader: Experience the love which fills your world,

People: For these are the great gifts of Christmas. Amen.

Prayer For Illumination

Angel voices are sometimes so soft, Lord. Help us to hear now, as the word is read, as the sermon is offered, as these voices join to sing. Help us to hear the flutter of angel wings, and the good news of the possibility of new birth. Amen.

Emmanuel

Call To Worship

Leader: Wonderful Counselor,

People: Who leads and guides us with righteous wisdom;

Leader: Mighty God,

People: Whose power is unconquerable and whose ways are good;

Leader: Everlasting Father,

People: Whose tenderness and love are unsurpassed;

Leader: Prince of Peace,

People: Who rains peace on those who open their hearts;
Leader: Come be with us now,
People: As we worship you for all you are and all you do.
Leader: Come, let us worship God!

Prayer Of Confession

Leader: There she stood, in the middle of the mall, the Christmas season whirling about her with carols playing in the background and children sitting with Santa, bright packages tucked under arms, people laughing. And she realized that the joy of the season was around her, but not in her.

People: Lord, we love Christmas! There's nothing wrong with that. But we want to pray today that we would learn that your birth is more than a cause for a yearly celebration.

Leader: It is a cause for eternal gratitude, permanent peace, and deep joy that cannot be held captive by a time of year or a set of circumstances.

People: May Christmas, this year, bring us more grateful hearts, a sturdier personal peace, and a joy that is a little deeper than ever before. Amen.

Little Bethlehem

Call To Worship

Leader: Just a little town it was, notable only for its insignificance,

People: A place called Bethlehem.

Leader: "Never heard of it!" would have been the response of most people of the time.

People: But it was to that obscure little town of Bethlehem that God decided to send a Son.

Leader: And from those humble beginnings, grew a man whose life shone with love,

People: And whose death opened the doors to eternity.

Leader: Just a small church, notable mainly for its insignificance;

People: A Presbyterian* church in Fairview.*

*Substitute local information

64

Leader: "Never heard of it!" is what most will say when they hear the name.
People: **But it is to us, in this ordinary little church, that God has sent the Son.**
Leader: And in this place, as we become like him, our lives will shine with love.
People: **And, as we give of ourselves, others will find their way to the gates of heaven.**
Leader: Let us praise the God who works through the small. Amen.

Prayer Of Confession

God, forgive us for thinking that we are too small, too insignificant, too ordinary for you to work through us. Forgive us for leaving your work to the great and the gifted. For in truth, you have gifted each of us. It's just that some gifts receive more recognition than others. But, we are not called to recognition. We are called to service, to serve as Jesus served, passionately, fully, humbly, sacrificially. Help us serve as he served. Amen.

Messiah
Call To Worship
Leader: Messiah, Christ, Anointed One, Savior;
People: **King of kings and Lord of lords;**
Leader: Wonderful Counselor, Mighty God, Prince of Peace,
People: **Everlasting Father, the great I Am;**
Leader: Fire on the mountain, thunder above the storm;
People: **Creator, Ruler, Judge;**
Leader: Abba, Daddy, tender Potter molding the clay;
People: **Gracious God, Forgiver, Lover of us all.**
Leader: How can we not worship him who is majesty, splendor, and glory?
People: **How can we not?**
Leader: Let us worship him!

Prayer Of Confession
Leader: Who needs a messiah? Not me!
People: **Yeah, saviors are for the weak. We have no need of a savior.**

65

Leader: That's the way the world thinks.

People: But not us, definitely not us.

Leader: Really? I wonder. I wonder if we passionately believe we need his salvation.

People: Hey! We come to church, don't we?

Leader: Yes, we do, but why? Do we come because we are grateful for his love and forgiveness, and our hearts want to sing to him with thanksgiving? Do we come because we ache to know him better? Do we come because it's a habit, because we think we should, because ... we don't know why?

People: Lord, why are we here? You know our hearts better than we do ourselves. Examine them. Cleanse them, that we may hunger for your truth, and rejoice at your gift of salvation! Amen.

Calls To Worship

Christmas Eve

Call To Worship

Leader: 'Tis the night before Christmas,

People: And in homes, one and all,

Leader: There will be giggles and laughter,

People: And folks having a ball.

Leader: And stockings will be hung,

People: In this place and that;

Leader: Awaiting their fill

People: From Santa's big heavy sack.

Leader: And while we sleep awaiting the first Christmas light,

People: The angels will sing their sweet song in the night;

Leader: Of the birth of the Savior, long ago, far away,

People: Of how he lay in a manger, asleep on the hay;

Leader: Of the love that he offers to you and to me,

People: Of the love we can take, of the love that is free.

Leader: For, you see, Christmas is more than stockings and toys,

People: More than presents for girls, and packages for boys.
Leader: It is love from on high that breaks all the chains,
People: That hold us so tight and cause us such pain.
Leader: So go home and hang stockings, and place presents with care, but before you lay down, say one little prayer:
People: Dear Jesus, sweet babe, angel of love,
Touch our tired hearts with God's power above,
Leader: And fill us this night, this one special night,
With the joy of new birth, and the thrill of your light.
People: And when the dawn comes tomorrow, Christmas morn,
Leader: We'll live, and laugh, and love! We too, reborn!

Christmas Presents
Call To Worship
Leader: Just one more week! Seven more days until Christmas!
People: We can't wait.
Leader: Me either! I want to pull off those ribbons and open up those packages to see what I got.
People: Yes, we do love Christmas morning.
Leader: Yeah, digging through my stocking, opening presents, trying on new clothes, playing new games;
People: It truly is the most wonderful day of the year.
Leader: But did you ever think about what Christmas would be like with no presents?
People: Are you kidding? It wouldn't be Christmas then.
Leader: But if Christmas is really about love then maybe you don't need the presents.
People: We like the presents though.
Leader: Me, too. But maybe we don't need them. Maybe we just need to tell the people in our lives how much we love them. Maybe hugs, and kisses, and gratitude, and smiles, and laughter around the dinner table are more important than presents.
People: Maybe they're the best presents.
Leader: Yeah, and it all starts with Love,
People: That came down from heaven to Bethlehem.

Leader: So, let's celebrate the Lover who gave the greatest Love Gift ever. Let's worship God.
People: Hallelujah. Amen.

Prayers Of Confession

Recognizing God
Prayer Of Confession
Leader: O God, the prophet proclaims, the angels announce, the star lights the way,
People: But still we ask, "Where?"
Leader: We keep looking for the magnificent, the powerful, the amazing,
People: Still not recognizing that you meet us in the simple, the quiet, the beautiful.
Leader: The fellowship of a friend,
　　　The love of a good man or woman,
　　　　The peace of right living,
　　　　　A flower, the sun-glistened snow,
　　　　　　The coo of a baby.
People: Keep us alert, O Lord, to recognize you. Amen.

Too Busy
Prayer Of Confession
Leader: O Lord, we know the child has been born;
People: But we are too busy to come see and adore.
Leader: We hear that glad tidings of joy accompanied his arrival;
People: But we are too busy to listen closely.
Leader: We've been told that he embodies God's profound love for us;
People: But we are too busy to taste his love and have our hearts warmed and filled.
Leader: Dear Father, this Advent, slow us down, that we might see and worship, hear and rejoice, taste and be filled with his love. Amen.

Waiting

Prayer Of Confession

Leader: Lord, the problem is, we just aren't very good at waiting.

People: We want it now. We long for it now,

Leader: For your arrival in our lives, in our world;

People: For the beginning of the kingdom where all the hatred, selfishness, and discord of our world

Leader: Is replaced by love, freedom, joy, and harmony.

People: We want it so bad we can taste it.

Leader: And sometimes, in our impatience, we give up on you, or try to make it happen ourselves.

People: Help us to learn to entrust ourselves and our world to you.

Leader: Help us to know that you are in control, and to wait humbly the coming of our King, Jesus Christ.

People: Help us, Lord, to be patient! Amen.

Chapter 4

Lent And Easter Liturgies

Collections
(Call To Worship, Prayer Of Confession with Assurance Of Pardon)

Lent — Barren Field
Call To Worship

Leader: The two of them, the young boy and his father, walked through field after field, each one drier than the last.

People: The beans were brittle, the corn crumbling, the harvest was ruined.

Leader: They were sadly silent until father said to worried son, "Fear not, God is good."

People: And the lesson was well learned.

Leader: Many years passed. Father said to son from his bed of death, "I have sinned great sins."

People: Son said to worried father, "Fear not, God is good."

Leader: Lent is a barren field.

People: It is a soul sorrowful over sin.

Leader: But, "Fear not!" say the angels of the Lord. "For God is good!"

People: Let us worship him.

Prayer Of Confession with Assurance Of Pardon

Leader: Sometimes we are the lonely, lost sheep, bleating out a cry full of fear.

People: But you, O Lord, always find us and comfort us.

Leader: Sometimes we are the rich young ruler, turning away from you because the cost of following is too high.

People: But you never give up on us, pursuing us each day of our lives.

Leader: Sometimes we are Martha, so busy with this and that — leaving you waiting for us.

People: But you wait patiently, calling to us, "My child, be not anxious. Come sit with me."

Leader: Lord, forgive us for straying from your path and care.

People: Forgive us for turning away from you.

73

Leader: Forgive us our busyness that pushes you out of our lives.

People: And let us always remember that each day is a new start with you. Amen.

Lent — Through The Valley

Call To Worship

Leader: The days of Lent are long, and dark, and cold.

People: The journey of self-examination is arduous and often painful.

Leader: There is the selfish, unyielding, sinful heart to face up to.

People: There is the hardheaded, arrogant mind to deal with.

Leader: It is, Lent is, a slow descent into the depths of the hell in our souls,

People: A repulsive, frightening place.

Leader: However,

People: How we praise the Lord for his "however,"

Leader: However, our God, Yahweh, the great "I Am," walks with us through this hellish valley.

People: Hallelujah!

Leader: All the while making sure that we know he will never abandon us and will, in the end, lead us through the darkness and into the beautiful light of his eternal kingdom!

People: Let us praise our God who never abandons us! Who loves us always, and leads us home!

Prayer Of Confession with Assurance Of Pardon

Leader: Lord, if there is one sin we are guilty of more than all others, it is the sin of denial.

People: We pretend that we have no sin to deal with.

Leader: We masquerade as people who have it all together.

People: We avoid facing up to our self-centeredness by keeping too busy to think or pray.

Leader: And so we miss the real joy of being Christian;

People: The joy of knowing that we are accepted as we are;

Leader: The unsurpassed pleasure of being able to be completely ourselves, without putting on an act.

People: O Lord, teach us of your great grace that we might know the freedom of being fully loved.

Leader: For then, and only then, will we be able to fully love others. Amen.

Palm Sunday — Holy Week
Call To Worship
Leader: Finally, finally the Messiah has come!

People: Yes, I can't wait to see him.

Leader: Hey, there he is, riding into town on a donkey.

People: What kind of king rides on a donkey? *(pause)*

Leader: Well, there's your Messiah, dying on that cross.

People: What a pity, I really thought he was the one.

Leader; Me too, but I guess we'll have to wait a while longer yet.

People: I guess, for this one will soon be dead. *(pause)*

Leader: Hey, have you heard the news? They say the tomb where they buried Jesus is empty!

People: Yes! Some say that they have even seen him.

Leader: Could it really be? Could he really have risen from the dead?

People: I don't know, but I hope it's true!

Prayer Of Confession with Assurance Of Pardon
Leader: Lord, as we begin this week of celebrating the most fantastic story ever told, help us to believe.

People: Help us to put away those doubts that prevent the deepening of our faith.

Leader: Help us to open ourselves to the glorious possibilities that your death did indeed wipe away our sin,

People: That you did, in fact, rise from the dead,

Leader: And that your rising means new and eternal life for us. Amen.

Palm Sunday — Messiah
Call To Worship
Leader: O Look, look, here he comes!

People: Jesus, the one they say is God's Messiah!

Leader: Riding on a colt, as the scriptures say!

People: Hosanna to the Son of David!

Leader: Blessed is he who comes in the name of the Lord!

People: Hosanna in the highest!

Leader: Peace in Heaven and glory in the highest!

People: All creation celebrates his coming!

Leader: Yes, even if there were no people to sing,

People: The very stones would cry out in joy!

Leader: Come, let us worship our King!

Prayer Of Confession with Assurance Of Pardon

Leader: I was so sure he was the Messiah,

People: But now it seems not.

Leader: He let them take him prisoner,

People: Seemed powerless to stop them;

Leader: No call to arms, no rebellion,

People: No angel army came to his aid,

Leader: No miracle to set us free from this bondage.

People: Still the same old world, the same old life.

Leader: He must not be the Messiah.

People: We must look elsewhere for our salvation.

Leader: So we turn away, never thinking that the salvation he offers may not be one that changes our circumstances, or sweeps away our troubles.

People: No, this salvation changes not the world, but us.

Leader: This salvation loves us with an eternal love,

People: Frees us from the weight of our sin,

Leader: Enables us to be who he made us to be,

People: Makes us more than conquerors.

Leader: This salvation gives us peace! Praise God! Amen!

Easter — New Life

Call To Worship

Leader: We wait for God that we might be saved.

People: Let us be glad and rejoice in God's salvation.

Leader: God will swallow up death forever and will wipe away the tears from our eyes.

76

People: **Let us be glad and rejoice in God's gift of wholeness.**

Leader: God will take away all reproach and make a feast for all his children.

People: **Let us be glad and share our gladness with compassion.**

Leader: Let us dry the tear-filled eye.

People: **Let us walk with the weary.**

Leader: Let us make a festival where all God's children may taste the goodness of his presence.

People: **Let us worship God!**

Prayer Of Confession with Assurance Of Pardon

Leader: God of new life, we say that we believe that everyone who is in Christ is a new creation.

People: **Yet when we consider our lives, we must confess that this newness is not always apparent.**

Leader: Remind us that we can only be truly new if we trust you and walk in your ways,

People: **The ways of transformation.**

Leader: Fill us with your empowering Spirit.

People: **Help us to walk the way of transformation,**

Leader: The way that leads from pride to humility,

People: **The way that leads from self to others.**

Leader: Thank you for your enduring, cleansing forgiveness.

People: **Use that forgiveness to free us from the fears and selfishness that keep us old.**

Leader: And begin making us new. Amen.

Prayer For Illumination

Speaker of the Word of creation, speak a new word of creation into us today, and create in us a new spirit that yearns to be the people you made us to be. Bless your messenger and those who receive the message this morning. Amen.

Easter — Resurrection

Call To Worship

Leader: They sat together, the twelve of them, around a table, with their Lord, their hero.

People: And they broke bread together, and they drank wine together.

Leader: In the heart of Jerusalem, they ate,

People: In preparation for their deliverance from all that oppressed them.

Leader: But then their house of cards began to fall. Their hero announced his impending death.

People: He was giving up, throwing in the towel.

Leader: A frustrated follower sold him to his enemies.

People: He was captured and carried away,

Leader: A sudden, crushing turn of events.

People: Even worse, it was betrayal by a friend, by a kiss.

Leader: Worse still, it was the will of his own Father. And soon he was deserted and dead.

People: The dreams had gone, the hopes had fled, the enemy had won.

Leader: It was sorrow, and sadness, and tears.

People: It was the dark, dark night of the soul.

Leader: But it was also, unexpectedly, a step along the way through the darkness and into the light.

People: Sorrow is often a step along the way.

Leader: And this man, this Jesus, betrayed, beaten, bloodied, and buried, leads the way, shows the way for us all.

People: Come, let us worship him who pioneered the way through every darkness into everlastingly radiant light.

Prayer Of Confession with Assurance Of Pardon

Leader: I believe in the resurrection of the dead and the life everlasting! Amen.

People: Really? Do you really believe that?

Leader: It is kind of crazy, isn't it? I mean, people don't just die and come back to life a couple of days later.

78

People: **Maybe you just want to believe.**

Leader: Maybe. I guess sometimes I believe and sometimes I don't.

People: **Come on. Do you or don't you?**

Leader: I don't know. It's just that I've never seen a miracle myself. If only I'd seen one, then it would be easier for me to believe something that's so incredible.

People: **So, you don't believe.**

Leader: Lord, if we were honest many of us would have to confess that we don't believe.

People: **We want to believe, but we have so many doubts.**

Leader: We think, maybe he wasn't really dead when they put him in the tomb;

People: **Maybe someone stole his body;**

Leader: Maybe the disciples just wanted it so bad they had psychologically-induced visions of him;

People: **Or, it's just a nice story about new beginnings.**

Leader: We have all sorts of rational explanations which deny the one and only explanation that gives the whole story meaning;

People: **That you are a God of such love and power that you destroyed death by raising him from the dead.**

Leader: Lord, forgive our unbelief and deepen our belief. Amen.

Calls To Worship

Gather Around Jesus
Call To Worship

Leader: We have come before you, O God,

People: **Like those who gathered around Jesus,**

Leader: On a faraway hill, long ago,

People: **To find new meaning to our lives.**

Leader: We want our lives to sound in harmony

People: **With your song of love.**

Leader: We want to live with integrity and wisdom,

People: With a spirit of truth.

Leader: Do not disappoint us, Lord,

People: But allow us to know your presence and hear your voice.

Leader: Come among us, Holy God,

People: For we ask in the name of Jesus Christ. Amen.

God Of The Living
Call To Worship

Leader: Trudging, plodding, struggling, surviving,

People: O Lord, this is our life.

Leader: But we forget, our God is the God of the living, not the dead;

People: The God of Abraham, and Isaac, and Jacob,

Leader: The God who authored life,

People: The God who gives rest, and peace, and abundant life.

Leader: We trudge,

People: He empowers us to live triumphantly.

Leader: We plod,

People: He empowers us to prance.

Leader: We struggle,

People: He empowers us to be people of strength.

Leader: We survive,

People: He empowers us to sing.

Leader: Come, let us worship this God of the living.

People: And let us become alive in him. Amen!

Need For Renewal
Call To Worship

Leader: O Lord, your love is like the sun that shoos the snow and shows the life beneath it.

People: We wait for your sun, O Lord!

Leader: Your grace is like the rain that washes over the thirsty soil.

People: We long for your rain!

Leader: Your power blows like the breeze on which the birds soar.

People: **We pray for the lift of your breath.**

Leader: Come, Lord, grant us in this hour a bit of the warmth of your love;

People: **A refreshing taste of your grace;**

Leader: And a gust of the Holy Spirit to lift us up that our praises might fly to you,

People: **Our hearts might be light,**

Leader: And our strength renewed for the days to come! Amen.

Prayers Of Confession

Deserted
Prayer Of Confession

Leader: We read of how they deserted him and wonder how could they? But we know,

People: **For we are people very much like them.**

Leader: They deserted because he said hard things;

People: **Because he made them look at themselves;**

Leader: Because he challenged their traditions;

People: **Said God loved everyone, not just them;**

Leader: Because he showed them their sin and hypocrisy;

People: **And called them to die to themselves.**

Leader: They wanted the victory, the joy, the peace, but the pain and sacrifice were more than they could take. So they abandoned him, though they knew he spoke the truth, was the truth.

People: **Lord, forgive us for being too much like them, too easily discouraged to desert him and his truth. Amen.**

Discipline
Prayer Of Confession

Leader: Lord, let's face it. We hate discipline.

People: **We like being free to do what we want, when we want.**

Leader: We'd prefer there be no consequences for our actions.

People: **We'd like to be free from correction or chastisement.**

Leader: Lord, we often think we'd like to be left alone,

People: But in our hearts we know that would be unbearable.

Leader: We need you even when your presence means discipline and correction,

People: Even when your presence means painful self-examination and repentance.

Leader: Teach us to accept your discipline, knowing it is for our good.

People: Teach us to be obedient children following the will of a wise and loving God! Amen.

False Gods

Prayer Of Confession

Leader: Father, we admit that we are easily attracted to false gods who lure us from you.

People: The "god of easy answers" whispers that we need not accept the cost of discipleship, but only its joy.

Leader: The "god of busy schedules" tempts us to delay doing your will until tomorrow.

People: The "god of cozy friendships" calls us to love only those who love us, rather than building a Christian family for all.

Leader: Forgive us our bent toward false gods.

People: Hold us close in your love that we may never forsake you, but always serve you faithfully.

Leader: And when we go astray, never stop pursuing us, for you are the only God in whom there is life. Amen.

Good Friday

Prayer Of Confession

Leader: Where might we have been, had we been there?

People: We would have defended him! We would have stood by him to the last!

Leader: At least we would like to think so, but I wonder if I would have been so courageous.

People: Well, actually, I wonder too.

Leader: We all do. When injustice in the workplace rears its head, and we ignore it,

People: We wonder.

Leader: When a neighbor is hurting and we're too busy to reach out a hand,

People: We wonder.

Leader: When we are more concerned about our comfort than God's will,

People: We wonder.

Leader: So, where might we have been, had we been there?

People: We wonder.

Leader: Or maybe we're afraid to say, to admit that we may well have been in that crowd shouting, "Crucify him!" because he called us to a life that was — and is — uncomfortable;

People: An unselfish life of accepting and forgiving, of caring for and loving, of giving and sacrificing,

Leader: A life different from the world around us, a hard life. So we, in so many ways, shout, "Crucify him!" by our actions and attitudes.

People: O Lord, forgive us. Forgive us. Amen.

Practice Godliness
Prayer Of Confession

Leader: Practice makes perfect they say, and we agree.

People: So we practice!

Leader: Our golf swing, or curve ball, or times tables.

People: We polish our writing style, or guitar strum, or communication skills.

Leader: We practice everything, it seems, but for the one thing we most need to practice, godliness.

People: O Lord, we confess now our obsession with the secondary things of life.

Leader: Help us give more of our precious practice time to the true fundamentals,

People: **To being good parents, to faithfulness, to integrity, to prayer, to scripture, to love.**

Leader: In the name of our Savior Jesus Christ, we ask it. Amen.

Prayers Of Confession
with Assurance Of Pardon

Darkness

Prayer Of Confession with Assurance Of Pardon

Leader: O Lord, everywhere we look, darkness! We see the dark side of life,

People: **Poverty, hunger, hatred, grief.**

Leader: We see darkness falling on creation,

People: **Air, and rivers, and forests destroyed.**

Leader: We see the dark side of people,

People: **Their pride, their anger, their sin.**

Leader: Forgive us our blind eyes that see only darkness,

People: **And open our eyes to see all that is light and beautiful in your world.**

Leader: To see the laughter and smiles even where there is pain;

People: **To see the hands that reach out in love to bring relief;**

Leader: To see the grandeur of the littlest stream, and the glory of the simplest tree,

People: **To see behind all that is ugly in humanity, and rediscover the beautiful image of God in each person,**

Leader: To see beyond every dark, cold tomb, and gaze upon the eternal truth,

People: **That life is everlasting.**

Leader: And even the darkness of death cannot put out the light of life!

People: **Glory be to the Father who gives life,**
　　　　And to the Son who redeems it,
　　　　　And to the Spirit who sustains it.

Love

Prayer Of Confession with Assurance Of Pardon

Leader: It's not about money, or power, or influence.

People: It's not about looks, or physique, or fashion.

Leader: It's not about cars, or houses, or other "things."

People: It's not about buildings, or altars, or steeples.

Leader: It's not about security, or comfort, or ease.

People: Then what's it about, this faith of ours?

Leader: It is about one thing and one thing only, LOVE!

People: The love of the Creator who fashioned his world with tender loving care for us,

Leader: The love of a God who never gives up on us,

People: The love of a Father who forgives us,

Leader: And a brother, Jesus, who dies for us,

People: The love we have for each other in Christ.

Leader: Father, forgive us when we are about all the wrong things.

People: And turn our hearts toward the one thing we need most to do,

Leader: To love you with all our hearts, minds, souls, and strength,

People: And to love our brothers and sisters as we love ourselves.

Leader: This is the whole law! Help us live it, Lord.

People: Amen!

Suffering

Prayer Of Confession with Assurance Of Pardon

Leader: O God, forgive us for the needless and useless suffering that we have caused others:

People: The malicious comment or hasty word, the self-indulgence that ignores need, the violence we wish on our enemies.

Leader: Forgive us, too, for feigning suffering to win sympathy, For playing the victim and expecting special treatment,

People: For using our suffering, real or imagined, as an excuse for irresponsible behavior.

Leader: And forgive us for missing the opportunity to grow that often accompanies suffering.

People: **For though you do not enjoy our suffering, you are such a God that you can make use of it.**

Leader: We praise you that even in our suffering, especially in our suffering, you are present,

People: **Bringing good out of evil! Amen!**

Chapter 5

Liturgies For Special Days

Liturgies

After Christmas
Call To Worship

Leader: Well, the holidays are over.
Reality has come back around.

People: School is back in session.
Santa's packed up and left town.

Leader: The creche is back in its box.
The star is down from the tree.

People: The shepherds and magi returned home,
Christmas is tossed out with the tree.

Leader: But Christmas is not a day,
that comes just once a year;

People: It's a way of life,
to be lived by all who come near,

Leader: To the manger, to the mount,

People: To the cross on which he died,

Leader: To the cold, empty tomb,

People: Where death was denied.

Leader: A life where we're led
in pastures of green,

People: By tables of feasting,
beside streams serene.

Leader: No, Christmas is not just a day once a year,

People: It's a life, a way for all those who hear,

Leader: The fluttering wings of angels on high,

People: The laughter of shepherds far and nigh,

Leader: The hushed awe of the kings
as they kneel by the Son,

People: Who brings peace on earth,
for each day and each one. Amen.

Prayer Of Confession

Lord, we love Christmas, but we forget it all too easily. We leave
behind the gift giving, the happy giggles, the warm embraces, the

time taken for love. What we leave behind are the lives you want us to live every day; we leave them behind as if they're just for the holidays. Help us not to laugh when we hear it said that Christmas is not just for Christmastime. Help us to see that that is the everyday life you intend for us, that your Christmas gift to us is fullness of life, every day of our lives. Help us to see and to live. Amen.

Assurance Of Pardon
Leader: We may forget Christmas,
People: But the Christ Child does not forget us.
Leader: His birth proclaims a love like no other,
People: A love which will never die,
Leader: And will always be for you and me. Amen.

Mid-Winter Blues
Call To Worship
Leader: Come this morning and lay down your burdens,
People: The post-Christmas, mid-winter blues;
Leader: The fears that you'll never find another job;
People: The anxiety we have over our health;
Leader: The nagging concerns about our children;
People: The guilt and embarrassment over some mistake;
Leader: The apprehension that keeps us from taking risks that would bring us growth and joy;
People: The busyness that keeps us from you and each other, Lord.
Leader: Come, let us lay down our burdens and rest in the healing presence of our God.

Valentine's Day
Call To Worship
Leader: Well, here we are, middle of winter.
People: Christmas behind us, spring yet in the distance.
Leader: The weather is cold. The days are short.
People: Dirty snow, cloudy days, blustery winds, and some of us let the drear into our hearts.

Leader: But today is Valentine's Day.

People: A day to celebrate love.

Leader: For most, it will be a celebration of the beauty of human love,

People: With lace hearts, and candy, and flowers.

Leader: But for us, gathered together here this morning,

People: It is a celebration of the source of that love;

Leader: A reminder, in the midst of dreary days and darkened hearts, that God is love,

People: That his love has come among us,

Leader: That he loves us with love enough to spare.

People: And that, therefore, there is love to share.

Leader: So we say, "Get thee behind me, dark heart."

People: For even in the dreariest winter, the Son of Love never stops radiating the warmth of his love to us.

Leader: Let us worship our God, and celebrate his love.

Prayer Of Confession with Assurance Of Pardon

Leader: Dear Lord, we are a people who long to love, long to bring joy to the people you have gifted us with, but so often we fail.

People: We hurt those we love most.

Leader: Our words sting our children,

People: Our thoughtlessness wounds our friends,

Leader: Our selfishness scars our lovers,

People: Our disregard keeps you at bay.

Leader: Lord, begin in us the agonizing process of exorcising our selfishness from our souls,

People: Helping us become like you —

Leader: Joyful givers, liberated from the chains of self-concern.

People: Pierce our hearts today, with the freeing power of your freely-given forgiveness.

Leader: Amen.

Memorial Day

Call To Worship

Leader: Today is a day to remember in America,

People: Those who have gone before us and secured our freedom.

Leader: Today is a day to recall in America,

People: The heroic actions of the many who gave themselves to protect us.

Leader: But we, in the Church, have secured something greater than political freedom.

People: We are citizens of a land greater than America.

Leader: So, today is a day, in the church, to remember those who pioneered our faith,

People: To remember Abraham's courage,

Leader: And Moses' strength,

People: And the passion of David for his God,

Leader: The confidence of Daniel in the lions' den,

People: The loyalty of Ruth,

Leader: The zeal of Paul,

People: And above all, the love of the Lord Jesus.

Leader: Come, Christians, let us celebrate our heritage, by worshipping the God of our fathers and mothers.

Prayer Of Confession

Leader: O Lord, living in faith takes courage.

People: And on this day, when we remember the courage of those who gave their lives for freedom,

Leader: And those who laid down their lives for faith's sake,

People: We confess that our courage is lacking.

Leader: We don't stand up for what we believe;

People: We don't speak out against injustice;

Leader: We are unwilling to confront an evil behavior in ourselves or others;

People: We refuse to make the sacrifices necessary to be free from the grips of the world.

Leader: Help us find our courage, Lord,

People: To take up our crosses and follow you! Amen!

Father's Day
Prayer Of Confession

Leader: Lord, we fathers are often distracted by the voices of this world. We want to provide for the well-being of our families, and we hear those voices telling us that the way to do it is to provide nice houses, big cars, great vacations, all the conveniences.

Fathers: Father God, forgive us for listening to these alluring voices.

Leader: For in heeding those voices we ignore the one voice that guides us along the way to abundant life for our families, your voice, which calls us to quiet times spent with loved ones, and to playing the games of children, our children, and to romancing their mothers, and teaching them to pray and live righteously, and to know you.

Fathers: Lord, turn our hearts away from the things of this world and toward the eternal, toward you, that we might truly be men of God. Amen.

Assurance Of Pardon

Leader: The best news the gospel offers is that it is never too late to turn our hearts to God; never too late to start anew with our Lord and our families. Let's turn around and go home!

All: Amen!

Prayer For Illumination

Almighty God, let us hear now, as we turn to your word, the voice of our Father. Let us hear a word of encouragement, if that be what we need. Let us hear a word of challenge, if that be our need today. Let us hear your word of discipline if we have strayed. Speak to us now, as a Father who always speaks just what we need, and help us to hear. Amen.

Labor Day

Call To Worship

Leader: Labor, and toil, and striving, and work,

People: These we do day after day, month after month, year after year,

Leader: That we might gain success and respect,

People: That we might find love and acceptance.

Leader: But we come here each week to rest from our toil,

People: To find sanctuary from the striving,

Leader: To get a taste of love and acceptance not based on our performance,

People: To be embraced by other sinners seeking sanctuary,

Leader: To feel the soothing balm of the love of God wash over our souls,

People: And restore what the world tries to wring out of us,

Leader: Self-respect, peace, confidence, laughter, hope, joy, love.

People: Let us worship our God. Amen.

Fall

Call To Worship

Leader: Well, it's over, isn't it?

People: Yes. Summer is gone.

Leader: And I guess we must leave behind all its joys.

People: All the splashing in the pool,
> **and the ball games,**
> **and cookouts,**
> **and trips,**
> **and all the rest.**

Leader: And face the fall and the coming winter.

People: With their back to school,
> **and back to work,**
> **and the coming of the cold.**

Leader: You know, we say it as if life is only good in the summer.

People: Sometimes we feel that way. We live for summer.

Leader: But life is good all year, when we live in God's grace.

People: You mean, when the leaves blaze with color, and the nights are crisp and clear?

Leader: And even when the earth is bedded down for a quiet night in a glistening snowy blanket.

People: Life is good even then, you say.

Leader: For God is love, and with God, it is never winter, but always only spring and summer.

People: Let us worship God!

Prayer Of Confession

Lord, we confess that we are too stuck in our ways; that we think we know it all; that our beliefs are eternal and unquestionable, and our ways are right always and everywhere. We are so right that we sometimes close ourselves to the Word you would speak to us. Heal us of our arrogance. Humble us. Make us vulnerable to your truth. Amen.

Assurance Of Pardon

Leader: Isn't it amazing that failure and disobedience don't cause God to turn away from us;

People: That God's love bears and endures all the mistakes and rebellion we commit;

Leader: That in spite of our falling so short, God still believes in us and hopes for our joy;

People: And always, always works to save us and raise us to glory.

Leader: That is good news! Great news! Amazing news!

People: Amen!!